Whales

Written by Helen Depree • Illustrated by Rick Youmans

The whale is the biggest animal in the world.
Dolphins and porpoises are very small whales.

The whale lives in the sea. It lives in a big family called a school, or pod.

The whale is a mammal.
It has a backbone.
A baby whale drinks
its mother's milk.

The whale has no legs.
It has flippers
and a big tail
to help it swim.
Whales swim a long way
to find food.

Some whales have teeth.
Some whales have no teeth.
Whales eat fish, small sea animals and plants.

The whale has a blowhole on top of its head.

It breathes air through the blowhole.
It can blow water up high
in the air through it.
Some whales have two blowholes.

Whales make lots of sounds.
They talk to each other
in whistles and squeaks.

Whales are endangered.
In many parts of the world
laws protect whales from hunters.